12-5-05

it's all about mini albums

A Leisure Arts Publication by
Nancy M. Hill of

acknowledgments

It's All About Mini Albums is the sixth in a series of books written by NanC and Company and published by Leisure Arts, Inc.

Author: Nancy M. Hill
Design Director: Candice Snyder
Senior Editor: Candice Smoot
Graphic Designers: Maren Ogden,
                   Rafael Nielson
Photographer: Julianne Smoot
Cover Design: Maren Ogden
Copy Editor: Sharon Staples

Cover Layouts: NanC and Company Design,
              Tracy Weinzapfel Burgos

For information about sales visit the Leisure Arts web site at www.leisurearts.com

Dear Scrapbooker,

I simply cherish this mini album to the left that a daughter-in-law gave me at Christmas time. Receiving it was one of the great joys of my holiday season! I enjoy not only receiving mini albums as gifts, but also making them and sharing them with friends. Hopefully, with ideas from this book, you too will experience how to create fun mini albums.

Mini albums are the perfect gift! They are quick to make, are ideal for capturing a special event or subject in a few pages and will be treasured by those who receive them. Mini albums are also a great addition to your personal scrapbook collection. They are just the right size to capture memorable moments, trips, or focus on a loved one or hobby.

Don't be intimidated or think you need to purchase a lot of new products to create mini albums. They use the same skills and many of the same products as regular sized pages, but are just made on a smaller scale. The page dimensions featured in this book are 8 x 8, 6 x 6, 5 x 7 and other irregular sized mini pages.

This idea book is full of fantastic ideas and examples to spark your imagination. "Lift" the ideas from this book exactly as they are or copy the basic design and add your own creative touches. NanC and Company designs offer a wide range of options to choose from with helpful hints and ideas along the way.

Enjoy trying these great ideas and, remember, the best part is sharing your finished mini album with someone else!

Nancy

table of contents

you are always in my heart

CONSTRUCTION TIPS

1. A posterity mini album is one of the greatest gifts you can make for yourself or a loved one. Family and friends will treasure the pages for generations.

2. Cut a piece of burlap to cover a portion of a page. Cut holes in the burlap and then put into a clothes dryer to fray the edges.

3. How to make a paper quilt:
   a. Crumple patterned papers and spray with walnut ink.
   b. Iron to flatten and dry the paper.
   c. Punch out squares of the patterned paper.
   d. Adhere squares to cardstock.
   e. Machine or hand stitch around each square.

4. Print journaling directly onto linen fabric by trimming and adhering a piece of thin linen fabric to a sheet of copy paper with spray adhesive. Run sheet of fabric and paper through printer.

5. Embellish a mini page with a tiny mini album of photos.

SUPPLIES - 5 x 7 Album

Cardstock: Bazzill; Patterned Paper: Chatterbox, Inc.; Corrugated Paper: DMD Industries; Metallic Embellishments: K & Company, 7 Gypsies, Making Memories, Darice; Fibers: Darice; Nail Heads: American Tag Co., Chatterbox, Inc.; Moldings: Chatterbox; Eyelets: Making Memories; Snaps: Making Memories; Safety Pin: Making Memories; Halos: Cloud 9 Designs; Stickers: NRN Designs, K & Company, Pixie Press; Cut Out: Karen Foster Design; Label: 7 Gypsies; Floss: DMC; Ribbon: Making Memories; Envelope Template: Deluxe Designs; Punch: Family Treasures; Stamps: Hero Arts Rubber Stamps, Inc.; Ink: Tsukineko; Paint: Delta; Photo Corners: 3M Stationary; Font: CK Nostalgia

Designer: Marsha Musselman

posterity gift album

Your middle name came from my Mom, your Grandma because she is a very special person in my life. She is strong, funny, honest, devoted, kind, and compassionate. I am very grateful for the character traits she instilled in me and I hope you feel honored and proud to be named after such a great woman.

The love and devotion I gave
to my children,
I thought I could give no other.
But God handed me a pleasant surprise,
The day I became a Grandmother!

Gram's Love

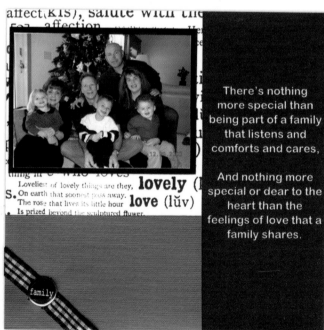

There's nothing more special than being part of a family that listens and comforts and cares,

And nothing more special or dear to the heart than the feelings of love that a family shares.

CONSTRUCTION TIPS

1. How to create a bronze coating on metallics:
   a. Rub metallic accents with embossing pad.
   b. Sprinkle with bronze Ultra Thick Embossing Enamel (UTEE).
   c. Shake off excess UTEE and heat with an embossing gun (use caution with heat in order to prevent metallic accents from bending or becoming deformed).
   d. While still hot apply a second coat and heat.
   e. Repeat with additional coats until desired look is achieved.
2. Alter ribbon by soaking in walnut ink. Dry ribbon completely and stamp with stamps and ink (make sure the ribbon is completely dry to ensure the ink won't bleed).

SUPPLIES - 6 x 6 Album

Cardstock: Bazzill; Patterned Paper: Memories in the Making, 7 Gypsies; Metallic Embellishments: 7 Gypsies, DCWV; Fibers: Adornments by EK Success; Stamps: Making Memories; Ribbon: Offray & Son, Inc.; Fonts: Lucinda Calligraphy, Gigi, Arial Rounded MT Bold, Times New Roman, Abadi MT Condensed

Designer: Tracy Weinzapfel Burgos

family photo shoot

CONSTRUCTION TIPS

1. Create a slide show by framing photos with slide mounts and adhering them to a strip of cardstock.

SUPPLIES - 7 x 7.5 Album

Cardstock: DCWV; Slide Mounts: Magic Scraps; Ribbon: Making Memories; Stamps: Stampin' Up

Designer: Ashley Smith

friends

SUPPLIES - 6 x 6 Album

Patterned Paper: Chatterbox, Inc., Anna Griffin, Karen Foster Design, Frances Meyer, Inc., Magenta Rubber Stamps, SEI; Envelope: Foofala; Letters: Foofala; Definition: Foofala; Tag: Foofala; Flower Brad: Making Memories; Ribbon: Michaels; Ribbon Charm: Making Memories

Designer: Melissa Chapman

SUPPLIES (RIGHT) - 6 x 6 Album

Cardstock: Making Memories, Bazzill; Patterned Paper: Memories in the Making; Patterned Vellum: Paper Adventures, Chatterbox, Inc.; Metallic Embellishments: DCWV, Making Memories, Altered Pages; Fibers: Fibers by the Yard; Thread: Coats & Clark; Flower Brad: Making Memories; Silver Brads: ScrapLovers; Round Buttons: Doodlebug Designs Inc.; Heart Buttons: Dress It Up!; Stickers: Altered Pages; Beads: Two Mom's Scrap n Stamp; Scrapbook Nails: Chatterbox, Inc.; Square Conchos: ScrapLovers; Ink: Stampin' Up, ColorBox by Clearsnap, Inc.; Ribbon: Michaels; Transparency: 3M Stationary; Adhesive: Magic Mounts, JudiKins, Magic Scraps; Fonts: Black Jack Regular, Bauer Bodini BT, Cricket

Designer: Susan Stringfellow

Amy, Caroline, & Ashley

Since we live so far apart, Amy and I have always sent each other holiday packages. For Easter many years ago, she started giving me handpainted glass egg ornaments. Now I have a beautiful collection. She also hand paints character eggs for Easter and Halloween.

Magic is when two friends walk in opposite directions but still stay side by side.

MEXICO '03

friend. 1. n. a person whome one knows well and is fond of. 2. an ally, supporter, a faithful companion. 3. a keeper of secrets. 4. a person with whom one can laugh or cry, share hopes and dreams. 5. one who is held in the most ... regard and highest esteem. i.e.: (Amy)

CONSTRUCTION TIPS

1. Print journaling and photos onto a printable transparency to allow the background to show through. Use brads, eyelets or stitching to attach the transparency to a page, or for an adhesive, vellum spray works very well. Be sure to follow the directions on the vellum spray in order to get optimal results.

2. Adhere beads to conchos with the use of diamond glaze adhesive. Double-sided tape can be used as an easy alternative.

book of friends

CONSTRUCTION TIPS

1. Jump rings are a great way to hang embellishments from key chains, fibers and frames. The jump rings allow the embellishment to jingle.

2. Combine different colors of embroidery floss to embellish layouts, write names and weave in and out of mesh.

SUPPLIES - 6 x 6 Album

Cardstock: DCWV; Patterned Paper: Memories in the Making, Making Memories, Close To My Heart; Vellum: Making Memories; Tag: Making Memories; Metallic Embellishments: DCWV; Brads: Making Memories, Lasting Impressions; Page Pebble: Making Memories; Rings: Making Memories; Acrylic Flower: KI Memories; Tiles: Tiles Play by EK Success; Rub-ons: Making Memories; Vellum Quote: DCWV; Floss: DMC; Date Stamp: Making Memories

Designer: Camille Jensen

animals are family too

SUPPLIES - 8 x 8 Album

Cardstock: Bazzill; Patterned Paper: Memories in the Making; Metallic Embellishments: Making Memories; Fibers: Fibers by the Yard; Mini Brads: ScrapLovers; Square Brads: Making Memories; Buttons: Dress It Up!, Junkits; Wire: Artistic Wire Ltd.; Mesh: Magenta Rubber Stamps; Glass Embellishments: Altered Pages, Halcraft; Cork Embellishments: Lazerletterz; Bamboo Clip: Altered Pages; Burlap Fabric: Hobby Lobby; Stamps: Dollar Tree, Close To My Heart, Stamp Craft, Disney; Ink: ColorBox by Clearsnap, Inc., Stampin' Up; Embossing Powder: Ranger Industries; Transparencies: 3M Stationary, Altered Pages; Adhesive: JudiKins; Fonts: Cricket, DC Recess Journal, Benderville, P22 Oh Ley, Two Peas in a Bucket Renaissance

Designer: Susan Stringfellow

CONSTRUCTION TIPS

1. Alter wire embellishments and words by flattening portions of the wire with a hammer.

2. Alter cork embellishments by stamping with a rubber stamp and inkpad, and inking the edges.

3. Create the look of a wax seal by heating several layers of Ultra Thick Embossing Enamel (UTEE) and while still warm, pressing a rubber stamp into the UTEE. Hold stamp in place until set (approximately 2 minutes).

the little book about me

CONSTRUCTION TIPS

1. Give an expectant mother a gift she will treasure: a baby gift book. Prepare the pages so the new mother only needs to add photos and facts.

2. Use snaps or brads instead of eyelets to hold down tags for journaling. This way the new mother can remove the tags to add journaling and reattach them without ruining the page.

SUPPLIES - 6 x 6 Album

Patterned Paper: Chatterbox, Inc., Memories in the Making; Tags: Chatterbox, Inc.; Jewelry Tags: Avery Dennison; Tacks: Chatterbox, Inc.

Designer: Leah Fung

school book

SUPPLIES - 6 x 6 Album

Patterned Paper: Chatterbox, Inc., Memories in the Making; Metallic Embellishments: DCWV, Memories in the Making, Making Memories; Tags: Chatterbox, Inc.; Snaps: Chatterbox, Inc.; Ribbon: Offray & Son, Inc.

Designer: Jlyne Hanback

CONSTRUCTION TIPS

1. Sand paper to give it a used look.
2. Don't be afraid to use the same photo on a page twice.
   Enlarge or shrink one of the photos to be an accent.

character quiet book

SUPPLIES - 8 x 8 Album

Cardstock: Bazzill; Tags: DCWV, Making Memories; Fiber: Fibers by the Yard; Brads: Making Memories; Staples: Making Memories; Stickers: Sticker Studio, Phrase Café by EK Success, Me & My Big Ideas, Chatterbox, Inc., Shotz by Creative Imaginations; Mesh: Magic Scraps; Photo Flips: Provo Craft, Making Memories; Envelope: EK Success; Pen: ZIG by EK Success

Designer: Sam Cousins

CONSTRUCTION TIPS

1. A quiet book is a great way to keep children (and many adults) entertained. Create your own quiet book with interactive pages that teach about color, the alphabet and texture. Choose elements that can be removed or flipped through to keep a child looking for more.

2. Create a unique background by adhering square photos directly next to one another on a piece of cardstock. Cover the photos with vellum and use as a background for your scrapbook page.

3. Add another dimension to your scrapbook pages by having envelopes, pockets and flip charts reveal hidden journaling and photos. Not only is it fun to remove an object from its holding place or lift a portion of a page to reveal what's underneath, but it's also a great way to add more journaling and photos to a mini page.

4. Gather inspiration and ideas from many different sources. The inspiration for this cover came from a daily newspaper.

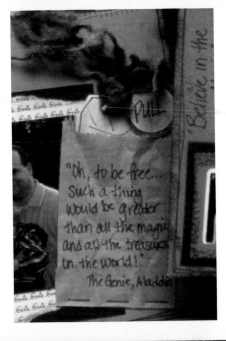

a year in the life of twins

CONSTRUCTION TIPS

1. Use the lines of a patterned paper to mat a photo without cutting extra paper.
2. Finish off a page by inking and distressing the edges of the paper. Simply brush an inkpad over the edges and, occasionally, across the inside of the pages.
3. Torn paper adds a nice texture to any layout.

SUPPLIES - 8 x 8 Album

Cardstock: Bazzill; Patterned Paper: Memories in the Making; Metallic Mesh: Making Memories; Stickers: Memories in the Making; Ribbon Charm: Making Memories; Ribbon: Making Memories; Font: Adler

Designer: Tracy Weinzapfel Burgos

CONSTRUCTION TIPS (RIGHT)

1. Simple pages really put the focus on great photos.

SUPPLIES (RIGHT) - 6 x 6 Album

Cardstock: Bazzill; Patterned Paper: DCWV; Metal Tags: Making Memories; Brads: Making Memories

Designer: Miranda Isenberg

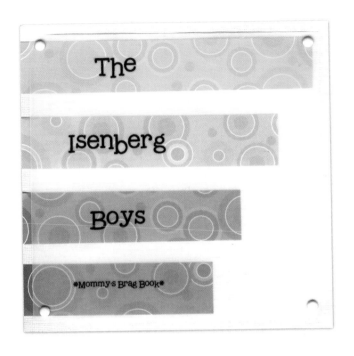

The
Isenberg
Boys

Mommy's Brag Book

Connor

Carter

Cameron

the isenberg boys

tin of photos

CONSTRUCTION TIPS

1. How to make a tin of photos:
   a. Adorn the outside of the tin.
   b. Punch out cardstock circles, just smaller than the diameter of the tin, with a circle punch.
   c. Trim a ribbon to 20 inches long.
   d. Sandwich the ribbon in-between two cardstock circles. Repeat, spacing the circles 2 inches apart from each other.
   e. Adorn circles with photos and other embellishments.
   f. Wrap ribbon around all of the circles and place inside the decorated tin.

SUPPLIES - 2.75 Diameter Album

Cardstock: Bazzill; Die Cut: Paper House Productions; Stickers: Paper House Productions; Ribbon: Jo-Ann; Stamps: Stampa Rosa, PSX Design; Ink: ColorBox by Clearsnap, Inc.; Embossing Powder: Stampendous!; Fonts: Two Peas in a Bucket Ditzy, Garamouche

Designer: Wendy Malichio

CONSTRUCTION TIPS

1. Make a two-sided mini accordion book. One side can document your childhood and the other your adult life. Tie both sides together with the same color palette and black and white or sepia photos.

SUPPLIES - 3.5 x 4 Album

Patterned Paper: K & Company, Karen Foster Design, 7 Gypsies; Tags: The Rusty Pickle; Metallic Embellishments: K & Company, Making Memories; Fibers: Adornments by EK Success; Eyelets: Making Memories; Stickers: K & Company, Karen Foster Design; Ribbon: Offray & Son, Inc.; Stamps: PSX Design; Felt: Offray & Son, Inc.

Designer: Melissa Fortenberry

a girl's dream

CONSTRUCTION TIPS

1. Emphasize a portion of a photo by encircling that area with a metallic accent. This can also be accomplished by tearing a window in vellum.

SUPPLIES - 6 x 6 Album

Cardstock: Bazzill; Patterned Paper: Ever After Scrapbook Co., Frances Meyer, Inc.; Metallic Embellishments: DCWV; Eyelets: Making Memories; Stickers: Chatterbox, Inc., Shotz by Creative Imaginations, Doodlebug Designs Inc.; Rub-ons: Making Memories; Soccer Balls: Card Connection

Designer: Tarri Botwinski

lily's book
of fun

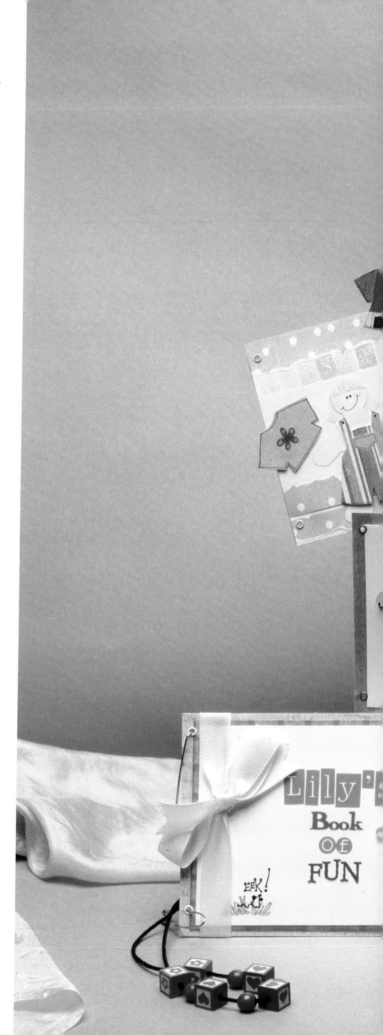

CONSTRUCTION TIPS

1. Assemble a book of fun for children. Make the book interactive with games and challenges on each page. Create a doll to be dressed with clothes made from patterned paper. Attach felt flowers to buttons to create a garden and even learn about animals by flipping up hinges.

2. Laminate pages that will last through the years and that will clean up easily with spills.

3. Place a magnetic piece of white erase board for an interactive page (magnetic because it is thicker and will hold up better). Cut the board the same size as the other pages in the book and attach border stickers around the edges.

SUPPLIES - 5 x 7 Album

Cardstock: DCWV, Making Memories; Patterned Paper: Memories in the Making; Pockets: Xyron, Inc., 3L Corp.; Concho: Scrapworks; Brads: Lasting Impressions; Stickers: Making Memories; Paper Doll and Clothes Template: EK Success; Stamps: Hero Arts Rubber Stamps, Inc., Simply Stamped; Fonts: CK Eight Ball, CK Constitution, CK Blackout, CK Academia

Designer: Camille Jensen

the top 10 reasons i love you

CONSTRUCTION TIPS

1. Use colors from your photos to create color schemes for your layouts.
2. Use a sewing machine to stitch pieces of paper together. Be sure to check the tension on a scrap piece of paper before sewing directly onto your background.

the **inn cence** of childhood that I see in you

SUPPLIES - 8 x 8 Album

Patterned Paper: KI Memories, Chatterbox, Inc., Memories in the Making, Paperfever Inc.; Brads: Lasting Impressions; Token: Doodlebug Designs Inc.; Bookplate: KI Memories; Alphabet Charm: Making Memories; Acrylic Frame: Heidi Grace Designs; Stamps: Hero Arts Rubber Stamps, Inc.; Ink: Stampin' Up; Fonts: Two Peas in a Bucket Hot Chocolate, Two Peas in a Bucket Grandpa, Two Peas in a Bucket Kipper, Two Peas in a Bucket Loose Curls, Two Peas in a Bucket Ragtag

Designer: Miranda Isenberg

the laughter that is like music to my heart

abc scripture
album

CONSTRUCTION TIPS

1. Generate a continuous feel throughout a book by using the same background paper, border strip and title format on each page.

2. Make an ABC scripture album with leftover photos and your favorite scriptures.

SUPPLIES - 8 x 8 Album

Cardstock: Paper Garden; Patterned Paper: Anna Griffin; Beads: Bead Heaven; Wire: Making Memories; Stickers: Mrs. Grossmans; Woodchips: Scrapfindings; Fresh Cuts: Rebecca Sower

Designer: Maegan Hall

my book of firsts

CONSTRUCTION TIPS

1. Create background by applying ink to make-up sponges and sponging white cardstock. Sprinkle clear embossing powder over sponged background and heat with an embossing gun. Repeat embossing steps until desired shine is achieved.

SUPPLIES - 8 x 8 Album

Patterned Paper: Memories in the Making; Metallic Embellishments: Scrap-Ease; Stickers: Wordsworth Stamps; Punches: Marvy Uchida; Ribbon: Making Memories; Stamps: Making Memories; Ink: Tsukineko; Pens: Pentel

Designer: Tracy Weinzapfel Burgos

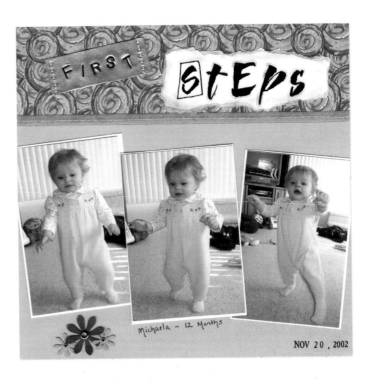

the bride

The Bride

A Selection of
Candid
Photographs

SUPPLIES - 5 x 7 Album

Cardstock: Chatterbox, Inc.; Patterned Paper: Chatterbox, Inc.; Tag: Chatterbox,
Inc.; Snaps: Chatterbox, Inc.; Stickers: Chatterbox, Inc.; Ribbon: 7 Gypsies

Designer: Tarri Botwinski

CONSTRUCTION TIPS

1. How to tear and curl paper:
   a. Dampen area of paper to be torn with water and tear.
   b. Make sure the tear is still damp and curl paper back. Continue rolling paper with your fingertips until desired curl is achieved.
   c. When the paper dries the curl will remain.
2. Make delicate titles and letters by reverse printing (in a photo manipulation program) onto a sheet of paper. Cut out the letters with an exacto knife.

love \lúv\ vb 1 a : to hold dear : CHERISH

Prayers

bryan & camille

SUPPLIES - 8 x 8 Album

Patterned Paper: DCWV, Memories in the Making, Susan Branch; Vellum: Memories in the Making, DCWV; Metallic Embellishments: DCWV; Silver Bug: American Crafts; Love Charm: Magenta Rubber Stamps; Brads: Lasting Impressions; Mesh: Magenta Rubber Stamps; Slide Mounts: Magic Scraps; Stamps: Hero Arts Rubber Stamps, Inc.; Date Stamp: Making Memories; Ribbon: Making Memories; Embossing Powder: Suze Weinberg

Designer: Camille Jensen

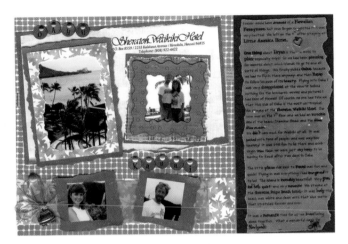

CONSTRUCTION TIPS

1. Create a fold out flap:

    a. Adhere a trimmed sheet protector or pre-made flap to the outer edge of the original sheet protector with double sided tape as if you were extending the page. Overlap the trimmed sheet protector three quarters of an inch.

    b. Slide a narrow page into the sheet protector with personal journaling on the inside when folded in.

2. How to paint a page:

    a. Use chipboard for the background instead of paper (so the background will not buckle from the paint).

    b. Mix two shades of green acrylic paint.

    c. Dry brush the background with the mixed paint and let dry.

    d. Brush a pearlizing acrylic medium over the dried paint for shine.

the great outdoors

CONSTRUCTION TIPS

1. Weave fibers through a background page to add texture and interest. Punch holes in the paper and thread fibers through to create a weaving pattern. You can use thick or multiple fibers by making a larger hole in the background.

2. Invite your children to write the journaling for a scrapbook page. It is fun to see children's handwriting and learn their perspective on the experience you are scrapping.

3. Create a microscope glass slide embellishment:
   a. Cut a piece of patterned paper the same size as a slide.
   b. Place dried flowers between the cut paper and the slide and adhere together.
   c. Heat emboss the edges of the slide with gold embossing powder.
   d. Finish by tying a ribbon around the microscope glass slide embellishment.

SUPPLIES - 6 x 7.5 Album

Cardstock: Bazzill; Patterned Paper: Memories in the Making, Chatterbox, Inc., Autumn Leaves; Vellum: Making Memories; Metallic Embellishments: ScrapLovers, Making Memories; Fibers: Fibers by the Yard; Brads: ScrapLovers, American Crafts; Stickers: Memories in the Making, Autumn Leaves; Cork: Lazerletterz; Chalk: Craf-T Products; Stamps: Dollar Tree, PSX Design, Stampin' Up; Ink: Altered Pages, Stampin' Up, Tsukineko; Embossing Powder: Stamps 'n' Stuff; Slide: Altered Pages; Leather Strips: Two Mom's Scrap n Stamp; Transparency: 3M Stationary; Adhesive: JudiKins; Font: Ancient Script

Designer: Susan Stringfellow

sandcastles in the sun

starfish

surfboard

sand castles

summer

seagulls

scallop shells

sand dollars

Sandcastles in the Sun

Kelly - 1998

CONSTRUCTION TIPS

1. Add texture and interest by gluing sand and seashells directly onto a tag or page.
2. How to make a gathered ribbon and button embellishment:
   a. Place gingham ribbon onto page.
   b. Plan placement of buttons.
   c. Gather ribbon where buttons will be adhered and tie with a piece of thread.
   d. Adhere buttons atop gathered ribbon with glue dots.

SUPPLIES - 8 x 8 Album

Cardstock: DCWV; Patterned Paper: DCWV; Mulberry Paper: DCWV; Tags: Sizzix; Metallic Embellishment: DCWV; Eyelets: Making Memories; Buttons: Dress It Up!; Stickers: RA Lang Card Company; Vellum Quote: DCWV; Stamps: Stamp Craft; Ink: Stampin' Up; Chalk: Craf-T Products; Adhesive: Therm O Web, Inc., Herma Fix; Fonts: Amazon BT, Synchronous

Designer: Brenda Nakandakari

cancun 2003

CONSTRUCTION TIPS

1. How to bind a mini book with fiber:
   a. Punch holes along the side of each page (create a template so the holes will line up).
   b. Sandwich the pages in-between the front and back covers.
   c. Line up the holes and weave the fiber through the book.
   d. Finish the book by tying the fiber off at the ends.
2. Print a photo onto a transparency to allow the background to show through and give the illusion that the photo is etched into the sandpaper.

SUPPLIES - 5 x 7 Album

Patterned Paper: NRN Designs, Bisous, Pixie Press, Making Memories; Metallic Embellishments: DCWV; Fibers: Fibers by the Yard; Brads: Making Memories; Stickers: Creative Imaginations, NRN Designs, Sticker Studio, Shotz by Creative Imaginations, Me & My Big Ideas; Vellum Quote: DCWV; Wax Seal: Sonnets by Creative Imaginations Stamps: PSX Design; Pen: ZIG by EK Success; Transparency: Magic Scraps; Adhesive: Creative Imaginations

Designer: Sam Cousins

autograph book

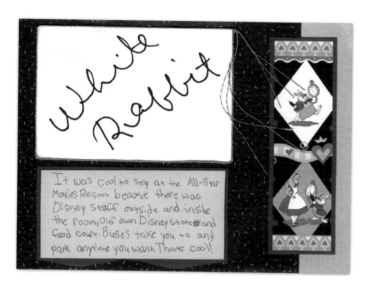

White Rabbit

It was cool to stay at the All-Star Movies Resort because there was Disney staff outside and inside the room, our own Disney store and food court. Buses take you to any park anytime you want. That's cool!

"I'm Late! I'm Late!"

The White Rabbit looked so cool up close. Alex said that I should have felt how soft his paws were. We left quickly to catch the monorail thru the hotel and around to the Magic Kingdom!

Mickey Mouse

Disney's ANIMAL KINGDOM

CONSTRUCTION TIPS

1. Create an autograph mini book to capture childhood memories from a family vacation. Leave a place for the children to journal their thoughts and memories as well as space for the 'celebrity' autographs.

Alex & Terk from Tarzan

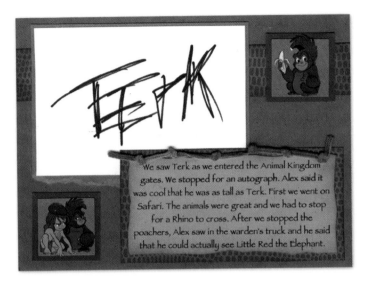

We saw Terk as we entered the Animal Kingdom gates. We stopped for an autograph. Alex said it was cool that he was as tall as Terk. First we went on Safari. The animals were great and we had to stop for a Rhino to cross. After we stopped the poachers, Alex saw in the warden's truck and he said that he could actually see Little Red the Elephant.

We Scare Because We Care

MGM

Sulley and Mike were really cool! Sulley was really big and he kept leaning on me! — Alex

Sulley and Mike couldn't sign autographs, but they were really cool!

MIKE

MONSTERS, INC.

alex AND SULLEY

SUPPLIES - 5 x 7 Album

Cardstock: Making Memories; Patterned Papers: Memories in the Making, Hot Off The Press, Frances Meyer, Inc.; Vellum: Making Memories; Metallic Embellishments: ScrapYard 329; Fibers: Fibers by the Yard; Thread: Coats & Clark; Brads: Making Memories, ScrapLovers; Stickers: Memories in the Making, NRN Designs, Stickopotomus by EK Success, Sandylion; Beads: Crafts Etc!; Bamboo

Designer: Susan Stringfellow

Clip: Altered Pages; Mesh: Magic Mesh; Punch: EK Success; Chalk: Craf-T Products; Embossing Ink: Stampin' Up; Embossing Powder: Ranger Industries; Ink: Tsukineko; Transparency: 3M Stationary; Adhesive: JudiKins; Fonts: Beach Type, Walt Disney, Adventure

christmas at our house

SUPPLIES - 6 x 6 Album

Cardstock: Chatterbox, Inc.; Patterned Paper: Chatterbox, Inc.; Fibers: Fibers by the Yard; Tacks: Chatterbox, Inc.; Nails: Chatterbox, Inc.; Rivets: Chatterbox, Inc.; Moldings: Chatterbox, Inc.; Frames: Chatterbox, Inc.; Stickers: Chatterbox, Inc.; Ribbon: Offray & Son, Inc.; Ink: ColorBox by Clearsnap, Inc.; Pen: Marvy Uchida; Labels: Dymo

Designer: Tarri Botwinski

CONSTRUCTION TIPS

1. How to make an accordion book:
   a. Cut background cardstock large enough to be folded in half to create two facing pages.
   b. Overlap the latter half of the first page to the first half of the second page and glue together. Then, overlap the latter half of the second page to the first half of the third page and glue together. Continue this process until you have as many accordion pages as desired.
   c. Make sure the folds alternate pointing forward and backward so the book can be folded properly.
   d. Finish the book by adhering ribbon horizontally to the back cover of the book. Leave extra ribbon on both sides to wrap around to the front of the book and tie in a bow on top.
2. Use a label maker for journaling.

holidays through the year

SUPPLIES - 6 x 6 Album

Cardstock: Bazzill; Patterned Paper: Carolee's Creations; Tag: DCWV, Making Memories; Metallic Embellishments: Making Memories, DCWV; Fibers: Fibers by the Yard; Brads: ScrapLovers; Eyelets: Making Memories; Stickers: The Scrapbook Wizard, Shotz by Creative Imaginations, Terri Martin by Creative Imaginations, Jolee's Boutique, Bo-Bunny Press; Rub-ons: Making Memories; Stamp: Making Memories; Ribbon: Making Memories, Impress Rubber Stamps

Designer: Sam Cousins

CONSTRUCTION TIPS

1. Manipulate photos with the use of a computer software program. Convert a photo to black and white and then add color back to certain portions of the photo.

2. Tissue paper comes in a variety of colors and patterns and can be used as a background for scrapbook pages. Attach the tissue paper to the background cardstock with a glue stick or other adhesive. Choose whether to make it smooth or crumpled.

3. How to paint metals and brads:
   a. Paint metals and brads with acrylic paint.
   b. Set with matte spray or clear embossing powder.

easter album

SUPPLIES - 6 x 6 Album

Snaps: Chatterbox, Inc.; Ribbon: Offray & Son, Inc.

Designer: Jlyne Hanback

CONSTRUCTION TIPS

1. Use paint swatches for journaling and as an accent on a page.

halloween album

CONSTRUCTION TIPS

1. Mat a photo with torn mulberry paper. Fold the top portion of the mulberry paper over the top of the photo. Stitch the flap of mulberry paper to the top of the photo. The stitching will hold the photo in place and provide a flap that can be flipped up to reveal journaling or other photos.

SUPPLIES - 6 x 6 Album

Cardstock: DCWV; Patterned Paper: Memories in the Making, The Paper Patch; Mulberry: DCWV; Metallic Embellishment: DCWV; Thread: DMC; Eyelets: Making Memories; Stickers: Memories in the Making; Adhesive: Herma Fix

Designer: Brenda Nakandakari

boo

CONSTRUCTION TIPS

1. Create your own sheet-protected 6 x 6 mini book:
   a. Fold 12 x 12 cardstock or other heavy paper in half horizontally and adhere insides together for the cover.
   b. Trim the tops of 12 x 12 sheet protectors to 6 inches tall. Cut the desired amount of sheet protectors (each trimmed sheet protector will hold 4 pages).
   c. Open the cover with the front faced down and place trimmed sheet protectors one upon the other with all the openings at the top. With a sewing machine, stitch straight down the center of the book to create the binding.
   d. Fold the pages and cover at the seam.
   e. Slide pages, just shy of 6 inches, into the sheet protectors.
2. Age metal embellishments by rubbing the metal with an inkpad. With a rubber stamp, stamp letters and images onto the weathered looking metal.

SUPPLIES - 6 x 6 Album

Cardstock: DCWV; Patterned Papers: Memories in the Making, PSX Design, Making Memories, Frances Meyer, Inc.; Vellum: DCWV; Metallic Embellishments: DCWV; Buttons: Doodlebug Designs Inc.; Slide Mount: Magic Scraps; Vellum Quotes: DCWV; Floss: DMC; Date Stamp: Making Memories; Ink: Staz-On by Tsukineko

Designer: Camille Jensen

the many reasons i love you

 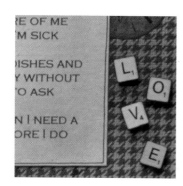  

CONSTRUCTION TIPS

1. Run faux suede paper through a printer to create an embossed leather look. Choose a font color a few shades darker than the color of the faux suede or leather to achieve the desired effect.

2. Hinges are a great way to add metallic accents to a page and also to allow a flap to be flipped up to reveal journaling or another surprise.

SUPPLIES - 5 x 7 Album

Patterned Paper: Memories in the Making; Metallic Embellishments: Making Memories; Snaps: Making Memories; Eyelets: Making Memories; Jump Rings: Making Memories; Buttons: Junkitz; Stickers: K & Company, Sticko by EK Success; Pen: Sanford Uni-ball; Font: Felix Titling

Designer: Leah Fung

super dad

CONSTRUCTION TIPS

1. Make a superhero book as a gift for a loving parent. Journal why the parent is like each superhero.

SUPPLIES - 6 x 6 Album

Cardstock: National Cardstock; Patterned Paper: Westrim Crafts; Eyelets: Making Memories; Buttons: Paper Bliss by Westrim Crafts; Stickers: Paper Bliss by Westrim Crafts; Die Cuts: Sizzix; Ribbon: Offray & Son, Inc.; Fonts: Comic Sans, Alor Narrow Condensed, Impact, Arial Black, Copperplate Gothic, Times New Roman

Designer: Mary Walby

Just in case my Dad doesn't know, Mom and I decided to show him how cool we both think he is. Mom says that we don't always celebrate the great stuff that Dad does and how much fun we have with him. This book was created for Father's Day in 2004, as told to Mom by Dad's little groupie. . .

My Dad is a SUPERHERO

. . . I Just Don't Know Which One!?*

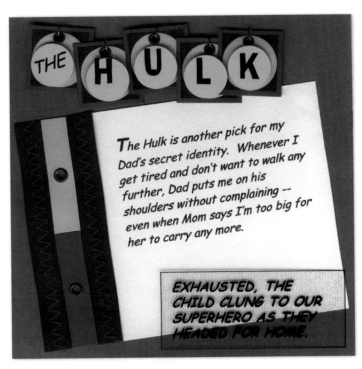

THE HULK

The Hulk is another pick for my Dad's secret identity. Whenever I get tired and don't want to walk any further, Dad puts me on his shoulders without complaining -- even when Mom says I'm too big for her to carry any more.

EXHAUSTED, THE CHILD CLUNG TO OUR SUPERHERO AS THEY HEADED FOR HOME.

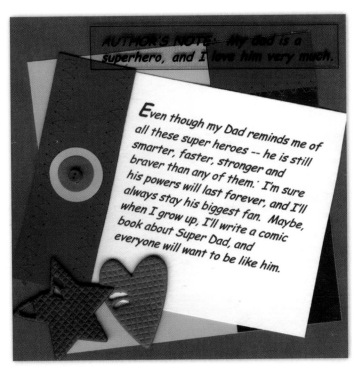

AUTHOR'S NOTE: My dad is a superhero, and I love him very much.

Even though my Dad reminds me of all these super heroes -- he is still smarter, faster, stronger and braver than any of them. I'm sure his powers will last forever, and I'll always stay his biggest fan. Maybe, when I grow up, I'll write a comic book about Super Dad, and everyone will want to be like him.

if flowers could talk

CONSTRUCTION TIPS

1. Create a mini book of your hobby. It is fun to imagine what each flower would say, if it could talk and journal these sayings.

2. Make a shaker box from slide mounts:
   a. Use two slide mounts of the same size and color.
   b. Trim and adhere a transparency to the backside of the front slide mount.
   c. Adhere the front side of the back slide mount to the page. Adhere foam tape atop that slide.
   d. Place buttons or other embellishments into the middle of the slide mount.
   e. Remove the protective covering to reveal the second sticky side of the foam tape and adhere the top slide mount with the transparency onto the bottom slide mount.

SUPPLIES - 8 × 8 Album

Album: Paper Pulp Products Inc.; Cardstock: Bazzill, Canson Mi-Teintes; Patterned Paper: KI Memories; Thread: DMC; Buttons: Making Memories; Slide Holder: Scrapvillage; Font: Two Peas in a Bucket Unforgettable

Designer: Betsy Sammarco

flowers talk . . .

Live life
to the

take time to
hang out with
your friends.

-Polygonatum
multiflorum

Learn to
bend before
the wind
breaks you.
-dicentra spectabilis

a year of recipes

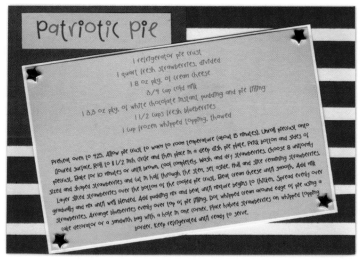

patriotic pie

1 refrigerator pie crust
1 quart fresh strawberries, divided
1 8 oz. pkg. of cream cheese
3/4 cup cold milk
1 3.3 oz pkg. of white chocolate instant pudding and pie filling
1 1/2 cups fresh blueberries
1 cup frozen whipped topping, thawed

Preheat oven to 425. Allow pie crust to warm to room temperature (about 15 minutes). Unroll piecrust onto floured surface. Roll to a 1 1/2 inch circle and then place in a deep dish pie plate. Prick bottom and sides of piecrust. Bake for 10 minutes or until brown. Cool completely. Wash and dry strawberries. Choose 8 uniformly sized and shaped strawberries and cut in half through the stem. Set aside. Hull and slice remaining strawberries. Layer sliced strawberries over the bottom of the cooled pie crust. Beat cream cheese until smooth. Add milk gradually and mix until well blended. Add pudding mix and beat until mixture begins to thicken. Spread evenly over strawberries. Arrange blueberries evenly over top of pie filling. Dot whipped cream around edge of pie using a cake decorator or a sandwich bag with a hole in one corner. Place halved strawberries on whipped topping border. Keep refrigerated until ready to serve.

Back To School Pencil Cake

1 pkg. cake mix (any flavor)
2 containers vanilla frosting, divided
red and yellow food color
chocolate sprinkles

Preheat oven to 350. Grease and flour 13x9 inch pan. Prepare, bake and cool cake following package directions for basic recipe. For frosting tint one cup vanilla frosting pink with red food coloring. Tint remaining frosting with yellow food coloring. To assemble cut cooled cake (cut in half length wise and cut one of the 2 resulting rectangles to give the look of a sharpened pencil) and arrange end to end on large baking sheet or piece of sturdy cardboard. Spread pink frosting on cake for eraser at one end and for wood at other end. Spread yellow frosting over remaining cake. Decorate with chocolate sprinkles for pencil tip and eraser band (directly under eraser, separating it from yellow).

directions

Line baking sheet with waxed paper. Pour popcorn into large bowl. Combine sugar, syrup in medium saucepan bring to a boil over medium heat, stirring constantly. Boil minutes, remove from heat, add peanut butter and green food color. Stir until peanut butter completely melted. Pour over popcorn, stir to coat well. Lightly butter hands, shape popcorn mixture into trees while trees are still warm, press red cinnamon candies in. Place on prepared baking sheet. Let stand until firm, about 30 minutes.

ingredients
6 cups popped popcorn
1/2 cup sugar
1/2 cup light corn syrup
1/4 cup peanut butter
1/4 cup red cinnamon candies
green food coloring

festive popcorn trees

SUPPLIES - 5 x 7 Album

Patterned Paper: Chatterbox, Inc., Karen Foster Design, Doodlebug Designs Inc., Memories in the Making; Brads: Lasting Impressions; 3-D Stickers: Jolee's Boutique; Fonts: Two Peas in a Bucket Lasagna, Two Peas in a Bucket Jack Frost, Chatterbox, Inc. Armymen, Two Peas in a Bucket Picnic Basket, BH Playful, Two Peas in a Bucket Renaissance, Two Peas in a Bucket Princess

Designer: Miranda Isenberg

CONSTRUCTION TIPS

1. Create a mini book of your favorite recipes so friends and family can share your traditions, as well as your great meals.

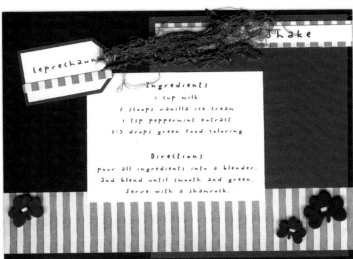

when grandma
was little like me

SUPPLIES - 5 x 7 Album

Cardstock: DCWV; Patterned Paper: Memories in the Making; Metallic
Embellishments: DCWV; Brads: Memories in the Making; Photo Corners:
3M Stationary

Designer: NanC and Company Design

CONSTRUCTION TIPS

1. How to make a horizontal mini album:

    a. Cut cardstock to 5 x 7 inches for inside and cover pages.

    b. Adhere a strip of brown paper to the binding side of each page (both front and back).

    c. With an exacto knife cut two slits at the left seam of the brown strip of paper on each page leaving an inch on the top and bottom of the page (use a template to make sure the slits all line up).

    d. Cut two pieces of ribbon and slide a piece through the top slits of all the pages. Tie the ribbon into a knot on the side of the book. Follow the same steps with the second ribbon through the bottom slits of the pages.

    e. Cut two more pieces of ribbon to tie the book closed. Adhere one ribbon horizontally along the midline of the inside cover of the book. Cut a vertical slit 3/8 of an inch in from the opening side of the cover. Thread the ribbon through the slit so the tail of the ribbon comes out the front of the cover. Cover the inside cover with a black piece of cardstock to hide your steps. Repeat this process for the back cover.

    f. Tie the two pieces of ribbon together in a bow to close the mini book.

christmas album

SUPPLIES - 5.5 x 7.5 Album

Patterned Paper: Memories in the Making; Charms: Memories in the Making; Micro Beads: Provo Craft; Foil: AMACO

Designer: Camille Jensen

CONSTRUCTION TIPS

1. How to make a vertical mini album:

   a. Cut a piece of corrugated cardboard to 6 x 12 inches, 6 x 7 inches and 2.5 x 6 inches. Make sure the lines of the cardboard are always horizontal with the 6-inch cut.

   b. Trim sheet protectors to 5.5 x 7.5 inches with the openings on the side. The reinforced edges of the sheet protectors should be at the top.

   c. Sandwich the corrugated cardboard and sheet protectors as follows: The long piece of corrugated cardboard right side down, sheet protectors with a thin strip (0.75 x 5.5 inches) of cardboard in-between each reinforced edge of the sheet protector, and the shorter piece of cardboard right side up. Make sure all elements are lined up along the top.

   d. Fold the 2.5 x 6 inch piece of cardstock to cap the top of the book and overlap onto the back and front covers.

   e. Punch two holes through the cardboard cap, covers, sheet protectors and cardboard strips. Make sure the punches are an inch in from the sides of the book and centered from top to bottom on the cardboard cap.

   f. String many threads of raffia through all the holes and tie in a bow on the front cover to bind the book together.

   g. Fold the bottom cover of corrugated cardboard forward creating two creases to allow room for the sheet protectors to be filled with pages. Make sure the top cover overlaps the bottom cover.

   h. Sew two buttons onto the book. Sew the first button, centered, a half-inch above where the front cover overlaps the back cover. Sew the second button, centered, a half-inch below where the covers meet. Tie a piece of string 12 inches long to the top button to be used to wrap around both buttons to close the book.

   i. Decorate the cover of the book and fill the sheet protectors with scrapbook pages

sources

3L Corp
(800) 828-3130
3lcorp.com

3M Stationary
(800) 364-3577
3m.com

7 Gypsies
(800) 588-6707
7gypsies.com

Altered Pages
alteredpages.com

AMACO
(800) 374-1600
amaco.com

American Crafts
(800) 879-5185
americancrafts.com

American Tag Co.
(800) 642-4314
americantag.net

Anna Griffin
(888) 817-8170
annagriffin.com

Artistic Wire Ltd.
(630) 530-7567
artisticwire.com

Autumn Leaves
(800) 588-6707

Avery Dennison
averydennison.com

Bazzill
(480) 558-8557
bazzillbasics.com

Bead Heaven
(410) 789-2153
beadheaven.com

Bisous
(905) 502-7209
bisous.biz

Bo-Bunny Press
(801) 770-4010
bobunny.com

Canson, Inc.
(800) 628-9283
canson-us.com

Card Connection
card-connection.co.uk

Carolee's Creations
(435) 563-1100
caroleescreations.com

Chatterbox, Inc.
(888) 416-6260
chatterboxinc.com

Clearsnap, Inc.
(800) 448-4862
clearsnap.com

Close To My Heart
closetomyheart.com

Cloud 9 Design
(763) 493-0990
cloud9design.biz

Coats & Clark
coatsandclark.com

Craf-T Products
(800) 530-3410
craf-tproducts.com

Crafts Etc!
(800) 888-0321
craftsetc.com

Creating Keepsakes
(888)-247-5282
creatingkeepsakes.com

Creative Imaginations
(800) 942-6487
cigift.com

Darice
(800) 321-1494
darice.com

DCWV
(801) 224-6766
diecutswithaview.com

Delta Crafts
(800) 423-4135
deltacrafts.com

Deluxe Designs
(480) 497-9005
deluxecuts.com

Disney
go.disney.com

DMC
(973) 589-9890
dmc-usa.com

DMD Industries
(800) 805-9890
dmdind.com

Dollar Tree
757-321-5000
dollartree.com

Doodlebug
Designs Inc.
801-966-9952
timelessmemories.ca

Dress It Up!
dressitup.com

Dymo
dymo.com

EK Success
(800) 524-1349
eksuccess.com

Ever After
Scrapbook Co.
(800) 646-0010

Family Treasures
(949) 643-9526
familytreasures.com

Fibers by the Yard
fibersbytheyard.com

Foofala
(402) 758-0863
foofala.com

Frances Meyer, Inc.
francesmeyer.com

Halcraft
212-376-1580
halcraft.com

Heidi Grace Designs
(253) 973-5542
heidigrace.com

Herma Fix
herma.co.uk.com

Hero Arts
Rubber Stamps, Inc.
(800) 822-4376
heroarts.com

Hot Off The Press
(800) 227-9595
paperpizazz.com

Impress
Rubber Stamps
(206) 901-9101
impressrubberstamps.
com

Jolee's Boutique
joleesbyyou.com

JudiKins
(310) 515-1115

Junkitz
junkitz.com

K & Company
(888) 244-2083
kandcompany.com

Karen Foster Design
(801) 451-9779
karenfosterdesign.com

KI Memories
(972) 243-5595
kimemories.com

Lasting Impressions
lastingimpressions.safes-
hopper.com

LazerLetterz
lazerletterz.com

Magenta
Rubber Stamps
magentarubberstamps.
com

Magic Mounts
(800) 332-0050
magicmounts.com

Magic Scraps
(972) 238-1838
magicscraps.com

Making Memories
(800) 286-5263
makingmemories.com

Marvy Uchida
(800) 541-5877
uchida.com

Me & My Big Ideas
(949) 589-4607
meandmybigideas.com

Memories
in the Making
(800) 643-8030
leisurearts.com

Mrs. Grossmans
(800) 429-4549
mrsgrossmans.com

National Cardstock
(866) 452-7120
nationalcardstock.com

NRN Designs
nrndesigns.com

Offray & Son, Inc.
offray.com

Paper Adventures
(800) 727-0699
paperadventures.com

Paper Garden
(210) 494-9602
papergarden.com

Paper House
Productions
(800) 255-7316
paperhouseproductions.
com

Paper Patch, The
(801) 253-3018
paperpatch.com

Paper Pulp
Products Inc.
91-792-535-1715
pppi.vze.com

Paperfever Inc.
(800) 477-0902
paperfever.com

Pentel
(310) 320-3831
pentel.com

Pixie Press
(702) 646-1156
pixiepress.com

Provo Craft
(888) 577-3545
provocraft.com

PSX Design
(800) 782-6748
psxdesign.com

RA Lang
Card Company
(800) 648-2388
lang.com

Ranger Industries
(800) 244-2211
rangerink.com

Rebecca Sower
mississippipaperarts.com

Rusty Pickle, The
(801) 274-9588
rustypickle.com

Sandylion
sandylion.com

Scrapbook Wizard, The
(801) 947-0019
scrapbookwizard.com

Scrap-Ease
(800) 272-3874
scrap-ease.com

Scrapfindings
(780) 417-0161
scrapfindings.com

ScrapLovers
scraplovers.com

Scrapvillage
scrapvillage.com

Scrapworks
scrapworksllc.com

ScrapYard 329
(775) 829-1227
scrapyard329.com

SEI
(800) 333-3279
shopsei.com

Simply Stamped
(925) 417-2264
simplystamped.com

Sizzix
sizzix.com

Stamp Craft
stampcraft.com.au

Stampa Rosa
stamparosa.com

Stampendous!
(800) 869-0474
stampendous.com

Stampin' Up
(800) 782-6787
stampinup.com

Sticker Studio
stickerstudio.com

Susan Branch
susanbranch.com

Suze Weinberg
(732) 761-2400
schmoozewithsuze.com

Therm O Web, Inc.
(800) 323-0799
thermoweb.com

Tsukineko
(800) 769-6633
tsukineko.com

Two Mom's
Scrap n Stamp
281-550-6155
twomomsscrapnstamp.
com

Two Peas in a Bucket
twopeasinabucket.com

Uni-ball
uniball-na.com

Westrim Crafts
(800) 727-2727
westrimcrafts.com

Wordsworth Stamps
(719) 282-3495
wordsworthstamps.com

Xyron, Inc.
(800) 793-3523
xyron.com

look for these published or soon to be published leisure arts scrapbooking idea books

It's All In
Your Imagination

It's All About Baby

It's All About School

It's All About Technique

It's All About
Cards and Tags

It's All About
Travel and Vacation

It's All About
Pets and Animals

10-20-30 Minute
Scrapbook Pages